ALPHABET EVERYWHERE

ELLIOTT KAUFMAN

ALPHABET EVERYWHERE

ABBEVILLE KIDS

An Imprint of Abbeville Press

New York London

For Jeelu, Sanaya and Asha

Photography: Elliott Kaufman
Editor: Cynthia Vance
Designer: Misha Beletsky
Production Manager: Louise Kurtz

First edition
10 9 8 7 6 5 4 3 2 1

Library of Congress Cataloging-in-Publication Data

Alphabet everywhere / photographs by Elliott Kaufman ;
[editor: Cynthia Vance].
p. cm.
Includes bibliographical references and index.
ISBN 978-0-7892-1115-6 (alk. paper)
1. English language —Alphabet—Juvenile literature. 2. Alphabet books—Juvenile literature. I. Kaufman, Elliott. II. Vance, Cynthia.
PE1155.A486 2012
428.13—dc23
2011053027

For bulk and premium sales and for text adoption procedures, write to Customer Service Manager, Abbeville Press, 137 Varick Street, New York, NY 10013, or call 1-800-ARTBOOK.

Visit Abbeville Press online at www.abbeville.com.

Preface

There is a world of letters just waiting to be discovered all around us—if we know *how* to look. Walking down the street, or hiking through a park, how many different forms can you find that resemble the alphabet in ways that are accidental? A sawhorse, the shadow of a bus shelter, or the old piers on a river become A's. An "M" is not only seen in the structure of a bridge, but on the backs of chairs, building entrances, bicycle racks or leaves. A "Z" can be found on a fire escape or garage doors, on motorcycles, or railings that bend. The discoveries are endless and yours to make. I discovered many of these "letters" near my home in New York City, using a simple digital camera. In the back of the book is a list of descriptions for each image; some have fancy architectural terms to describe the different kinds of details found on the buildings around us.

Start your hunt anytime, anywhere—and find all kinds of unintended shapes. Explore the world in new way and start finding your own alphabet…everywhere!

—Elliott Kaufman

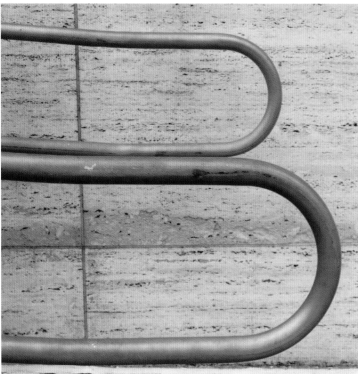

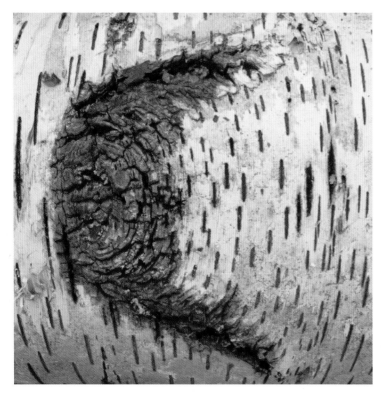

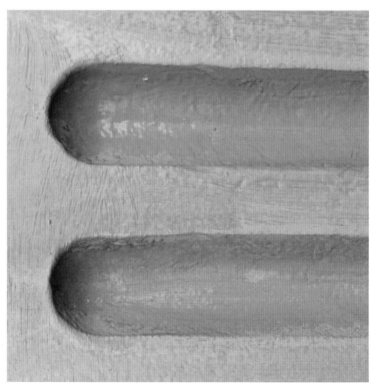

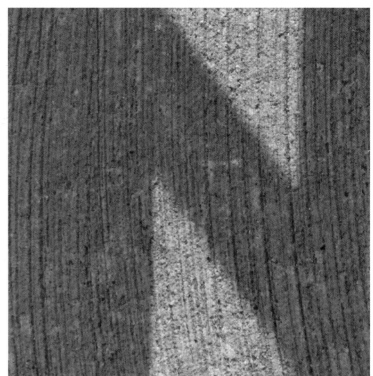

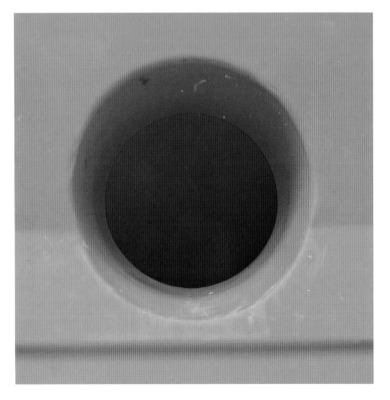

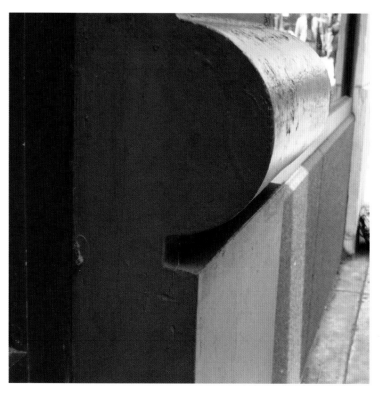

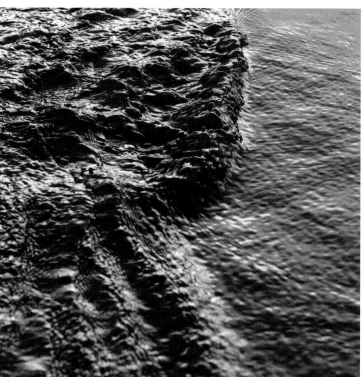

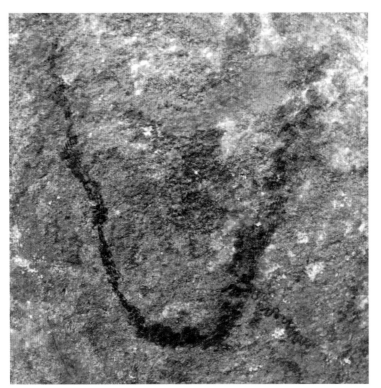

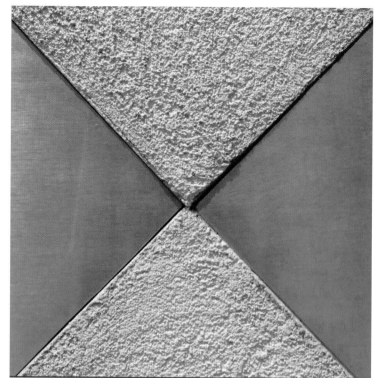

Index

F.
1. Shadows in a stairwell
2. Stair railing
3. Tree bark formation
4. Store entryway frame detail
5. Pier and pilings

G.
1. "C" clamp
2. Wrought iron fence ornament
3. Carved granite volute (decorative spiral shape)
4. Chain lock on fence
5. Carved limestone pilaster (ornamental column)

H.
1. Steel window guard
2. Concert hall balcony
3. Etched-in damage on birch bark
4. Wood molding on door
5. Scaffolding

I.
1. Shadow of window frame
2. COR-TEN (type of steel) slot in building exterior
3. Limestone façade pattern
4. Painted steel support
5. Steel I-Beam

J.
1. Ironwork door detail
2. Iron pipe
3. Copper handrail return
4. Carved limestone lion sculpture
5. Exterior wall-mount lantern

K.
1. Steel skylight framing from underneath
2. Subway station mosaic wall
3. Steel scaffolding
4. Aluminum curtain wall window frame
5. Crosswalk markings

L.
1. Shadow of overhang on brick wall
2. Hydrant pipe connection
3. Oxidized metal in granite rock
4. Park bench
5. Outdoor neon light sculpture

M.
1. Bicycle rack
2. Embossed brass building decoration
3. Climbing grapevine leaf
4. Grain silos
5. Bridge truss from underneath

N.
1. Cutting in granite rock formation
2. Shadow of scaffolding on sandstone wall
3. Heavy timber bracing
4. Painted steel handrail section
5. Chain link fence with green slats

O.
1. Tractor headlight
2. Sprinkler alarm
3. Temporary road construction barrier
4. Large hollow tree trunk in swamp
5. Carved limestone wreath

P.
1. Shadow of iron handrail return
2. Rough limestone corbel (stone projection)
3. Steel spring
4. Iron building façade base
5. Fiddlehead fern sprout

Q.
1. Contemporary streetlamp
2. Hollow birch tree branch
3. Wrought iron ring clamp
4. Basketball hoop
5. Public bench

R.
1. Cattle gate
2. Ocean wave approaching shore
3. Marquis suspension chain
4. Railroad shipping container
5. Shadow from truck

S.
1. Exposed tree root
2. Bus handrail
3. Decorative terracotta column
4. Formation in granite boulder
5. Ornamental brass door handle

T.
1. Raised limestone building panels
2. Stainless steel and granite office building detail
3. Wrought iron fence
4. Cast concrete building facade
5. Standpipe connection

U.
1. Pattern in granite rock with green lichen
2. "Lucky" horseshoe
3. Bicycle roller chain
4. Tractor engine belt
5. Metal staple

V.
1. Crevices in granite outcropping
2. Tulip blossom
3. Tulip leaf with shadow
4. Looking up at large soffit (overhang)
5. Split oak tree trunk

W.
1. Metal planter curb (raised edge)
2. Wake from a speedboat
3. Shadow on corrugated steel.
4. Marble steps
5. Steel pedestrian bridge rail and truss

X.
1. Wooden cross-bracing
2. Stainless steel and stone panel façade
3. Fire hydrant cap
4. Fallen tree branches
5. Metal braces on glass office building

Y.
1. Crotch of branching tree
2. Paving stone pattern
3. Siamese hydrant standpipe from above
4. Chain with lock
5. Figure from a monument sculpture

Z.
1. Loading dock roll down gate
2. Formation in marbleized bluestone
3. Shadow of scaffolding on sidewalk
4. Motorcycle shock absorbers
5. Old wooden silo door

ELLIOTT KAUFMAN is an architectural photographer who has traveled worldwide on assignment, and his work has been displayed in such venues as the Philadelphia Museum of Art, the Light Gallery (NYC), the Alan Klotz Gallery (NYC) and the Carrie Haddad Gallery (Hudson, NY). He has taught at the International Center of Photography, Long Island University, and Queens College.